JUSTICE SANDRA DAY O'CONNOR

JUSTICE SANDRA DAY O'CONNOR

by
Mary
Virginia
Fox

ENSLOW PUBLISHERS
Bloy Street and Ramsey Avenue
Box 777
Hillside, New Jersey 07205

CHAPTER II
LJHS-1984
92/OCO
525
10.68

Library of Congress Cataloging in Publication Data

Fox, Mary Virginia.
    Justice Sandra Day O'Connor.
    Summary: A biography of the attorney who on September
25, 1981 became the first woman justice on the United
States Supreme Court.
    1. O'Connor, Sandra Day, 1930-   —Juvenile
literature. 2. Judges—United States—Biography—
Juvenile literature. [1. O'Connor, Sandra Day,
1930- . 2. Judges. 3. United States. Supreme
Court—Biography] I. Title.
KF8745.025F69   1983   347.73'2634 [B] 82-8857
ISBN 0-89490-073-0   347.3073534 [B] [92]

Printed in the United States of America

10 9 8 7 6 5 4 3 2

1

Sandra Day O'Connor stood by a side door which led to the ornate marble and mahogany courtroom of the Supreme Court. This was a very special day for her, this September 25, 1981. She was to be sworn in as the first woman ever to serve on the highest court of the country. She would soon take her place as one of the nine justices of the United States Supreme Court.

Earlier that day she had taken an oath "to administer justice without respect to persons and do equal right to the poor and to the rich." This very private ceremony had taken place in the Court's conference room in the presence of President and Mrs. Reagan, the eight judges she would soon be joining, retiring Justice Potter Stewart, and her immediate family. As she had spoken the words of the oath, she had placed her right hand on two O'Connor family Bibles held by her husband John.

Now the formal investiture was to take place in

Chief Justice Warren Burger administers the oath of office to Sandra Day O'Connor. Her husband John J. O'Connor holds two family bibles. —*Wide World Photos*

the courtroom. The atmosphere was calm as she waited. The excitement had come earlier. Perhaps the most emotion-packed moment was the day she was told she was being considered for this position. That had been only four months ago. It seemed much longer. So much had happened to change her life since then. She had been interviewed by fellow lawyers, senators, a crush of reporters, and finally by the President of the United States himself. And all the time she had known that other lawyers and judges throughout the country were also being considered, any one of whom might be chosen.

This honor carried with it grave responsibilities and duties for the rest of her life. Was she willing to give up the freedom of privacy? She had her own family, a husband and three nearly grown sons, to consider. Never once had any of them voiced doubts that she would be chosen and, if chosen, would accept the honor. It could have been a frightening honor, weighing heavily on her shoulders, but Sandra Day O'Connor is a person who faces challenges with enthusiasm.

The Senate hearings, during which she had been questioned by friends and critics alike, had been almost unbearably tense. There had been those who had spoken against her nomination, and their voices had been powerful. To please everybody meant pleasing no one. But it was hard to hear the sharp criticism of some of her views.

Five hundred guests filled the courtroom beyond its four-hundred seat capacity. President Reagan entered from the opposite side of the room. Sandra O'Connor was escorted to a ceremonial chair below and in front of the court bench. This is the term used for the seats behind a long counter-like table raised a few feet on a dais above the courtroom floor. The ceremonial chair she sat upon was part of the historic tradition of our country's past. It had been used by the first Chief Justice, John Marshall.

When Sandra O'Connor was seated, her eight colleagues of the Supreme Court filed into the room wearing the robes of their office. The bailiff cried the traditional, "Oyez, oyez," and the ceremony began.

Attorney General William French Smith presented to the court the official document signed by President Reagan commissioning Judge O'Connor as an associate justice of the Supreme Court of the United States. Alexander Stevas, the Clerk of the Supreme Court, read the document aloud. Then Chief Justice Warren Burger called Judge O'Connor to the bench.

The oath she now took was the same that is required of all federal officials. She pledged "to support and defend the Constitution of the United States of America."

Charles Cornelison, the Court's chief deputy marshall, next helped Justice O'Connor on with the judicial robe she had brought with her, the same one

Chief Justice Warren Burger and Justice Sandra Day O'Connor stand with her father Harry Day, husband John, mother Ada Mae Day, and sons Brian, Jay, and Scott in front of the U.S. Supreme Court building.

she had worn when presiding over the Arizona Court of Appeals.

Sandra O'Connor then took her seat at the far end of the bench, which is the place reserved for the most junior justice. There she was seated next to Justice William H. Rehnquist, a friend and former classmate at Stanford University Law School.

There were smiles on many faces. Chief Justice Burger said, "Justice O'Connor, welcome to the Court. I wish you a very long life and happy career in our common calling."

She smiled and thanked him. Then she looked toward the seats reserved for her family. Her husband John and their three sons, Jay, Brian, and Scott, were grinning.

When the brief ceremony ended Justice O'Connor was ushered outside into a sun-filled inner courtyard of the Supreme Court building so that the press could take more pictures. Supreme Court employees who had not been able to get seats in the courtroom waved from the windows and the new justice waved back.

Everyone was in a jovial mood. Only her mother and father, Harry and Ada Mae Day, were more somber, though they must have been bursting with pride. Her father was standing at attention as if the solemnity of the moment was not to be broken. And yet he had never been all that solemn a person. Sandra had grown up in a warm, outgoing family where the atmosphere was rarely formal.

Perhaps it was the fact that their home was set in the rugged, bleak, empty countryside of Arizona, far from neighbors, that brought about a closeness the Day family has never lost. It was from her family that Justice O'Connor had drawn her greatest strength.

2

Sandra spent many of her happiest childhood days on the family ranch, riding horses, even roping steers. The ranch is a harsh 260-square-mile tract of dust and cactus on the Arizona-New Mexico border. It has been owned by the Day family for over a hundred years.

Sandra's grandfather, Henry Clay Day, homesteaded the land during the days when there were more Indians than white settlers in the area. He was a native of Vermont who headed West to make his fortune.

He was not like many penniless settlers who came to a harsh land without resources. To make a ranch profitable took a considerable outlay of cash, even in the 1870s.

Henry Day first settled in Wichita, Kansas, where he became a lumberman at a time when the settlement was expanding from town to city. He banked $50,000 in profits toward the day when they could be used for his own investment in a ranch and livestock.

Already he had picked out the land for his new home. There was nothing here in southern Arizona to remind him of the green hills of Vermont. The horizon stretched without limits. The sparse grass turned green only when an occasional rainfall dampened the cracked and rocky soil. Yet there was enough forage to sustain a herd of cattle if there were enough acres for them to roam.

It took a lot of hard work to dig wells and set up windmill pumps to fill water holes to keep cattle and horses alive. It was not an easy life. Only those with a strong determination survived, but it was here that Henry Day found a freedom and love for the land that his granddaughter was also to share.

He hired his nephew to go to Mexico and buy livestock. When the young man returned he was driving 5000 head of healthy cattle all marked with a B brand. That settled the problem of what to call the ranch. It has been known as the Lazy B ever since.

In 1880 Henry Clay Day moved his family to the small adobe house he had built on his land. Eighteen years later Sandra's father Harry was born. He was Henry and Alice's fifth and last child. Henry Day had built a one-room schoolhouse on the ranch for his own children and any of the ranch hands' families who wanted to use it. But he was well aware that the education available was not up to Eastern standards or those of the more civilized communities of the West. He finally decided to leave the ranch's management in the hands of his foreman and to head for Pasadena, California. That is where Sandra's father spent most of his early years, and where he graduated from high school with plans to enroll at Stanford University.

His plans were cut short when his father suddenly died. Another shock soon hit them. The family learned that they were about to lose the ranch. Money had been borrowed to increase the size of the spread and to buy more cattle to stock it. Poor judgment and poor management had brought about disaster.

Harry, the youngest in the family, was the one who was most like his father. He loved the land. Plans for college were canceled. He headed back to Arizona to try to work out the financial problems. Once the creditors knew the real owner was in charge, most of the problems were solved.

Thanks to the generosity of a prosperous El Paso cattle trader and rancher named Willis Wilkey, Harry Day was able to put the Lazy B back on its feet again. Mr. Wilkey did him another favor by introducing him to his daughter Ada Mae.

Sandra O'Connor says with a smile, "My father likes to say he met my mother when he went to buy some bulls and she was part of the deal."

This is far from the truth. Ada Mae was a very sophisticated young lady for her day. She graduated from the University of Arizona, Class of '21. She had a taste for high fashion which did not include denim or cowboy boots, and she loved books.

El Paso was a remarkably cosmopolitan city even in the 1920s. There was a fine library, a symphony orchestra, and an art museum. It did not, perhaps, equal the hub of culture on the East Coast, but it was more glamorous and polished than the cowtown it was falsely reputed to be.

Ada Mae had seen more of the world than this. As a sixteen-year-old, she and several of her school classmates, accompanied by their English teacher, had taken the grand tour of Europe.

There were many differences between the citified Ada Mae and the rancher Harry. Though he was no country bumpkin, having spent his early years in Pasadena, Harry still called the tract of near-wilderness which was the Lazy B, home.

Differences or not, a strong feeling of admiration and affection soon turned to love. Harry spent hours on the road commuting between El Paso and the ranch, a distance of some two hundred miles without superhighways. Finally the courting ended when the couple eloped to Las Cruces, New Mexico. The year was 1927.

Harry remembers, "We drove around half the

Justice O'Connor's parents, Ada Mae and Harry Day, at their ranch in Arizona. —*Wide World Photos*

night waiting for the courthouse to open." Then he pauses with a grin. "It was worth the wait."

Ada Mae moved into the ranch house Harry's father had built many years before. There were few luxuries; in fact there were few of the comforts most of us would consider essential today. The home was a four-room adobe house with no electricity or plumbing. Four ranch hands slept on the screened porch for a few years until Harry managed to build a bunkhouse. Ada Mae hauled water from the well until 1937, when plumbing was added.

It was some time before the kerosene lamps gave way to electricity, but Harry didn't wait for the public utility to string lines out to the Lazy B. He built his own generator to lighten the load of ranching and housework. It was a great day when the first switch was turned on. Still, this new power had to be used sparingly. When the washing machine was running, lights dimmed.

But the Days can brag of being one of the first users of solar heat in the country. Harry read about some experiments at the University of California, so he sent for a pamphlet that showed him how to lace pipes across a reflector to make his own solar heater.

It was primitive living, and yet the owner of 260 square miles of land with a total investment of many thousands of dollars could not exactly be described as poor. It was a way of life familiar to many of the ranchers—hard work, no frills, but independence. It was this need to feel beholden to no one that made them carve out their future in such an isolated, rugged part of the country.

Harry Day was well known and well liked in the area. He'd been chosen as a mediator in a conflict over grazing rights in the early 1930s.

Ada Mae was an excellent cook and a diligent housewife, but still she saved time for reading. There must have been plenty of time on her hands, for the distance between one ranch house and another made a neighborly social life all but impossible. The *Los Angeles Times* and the *New Yorker* and *Vogue* magazines were delivered regularly. Ada Mae's clothes were selected from the latest issues of the fashion magazines and bought by mail. She got to show them off occasionally when the couple traveled to the city for a stockman's convention, to visit family, or just for a vacation. Never once does her family remember seeing her in jeans.

Three years after their marriage on March 26, 1930 their first child, Sandra, was born. Ada Mae moved back to her parents' home in El Paso during the last month of her pregnancy to be closer to medical care and a hospital.

On the day Sandra was born her father was in a federal courthouse in Tucson, Arizona, battling lawyers from three states in a case that was to last ten

Justice Sandra Day O'Connor

years, concerning leasing government land for grazing.

"I don't remember telling Sandra that I wanted her to study law," he says now, "but after dealing with slick lawyers that long, I thought, damn, I'd like to have a little legal advice somewhere in the family."

Harry rushed back to El Paso to be with his wife and to greet his new daughter. As a very proud father, he was also worried about his family's immediate future. Harry suggested that Ada Mae stay in El Paso for a while until the baby was older, and he would commute back and forth when he could. He was afraid the rugged ranch life would be too hard on a new mother and baby.

Ada Mae did not approve the plan. "I missed Harry," she says, "and the cowboys needed me."

Around the time her daughter became a justice, Ada Mae was asked if it wasn't very hard to leave the comforts of El Paso with a newborn child. Her answer tells a lot about the Day family. Ada Mae thought for a moment, then said, "No, it wasn't hard. I just loved Harry so much."

Within a month she was back at the ranch full time.

Sandra Day O'Connor on horseback during a roundup at the Lazy B ranch.   —*Phoenix Newspapers, Inc.*

3

Sandra's earliest memories are of horses, cattle, and dust storms. But when she talks about her childhood, it is not with a sense that these were hard, lonely days. It is with joy and humor that she recalls the good times. Like her father and grandfather before her, she loved the land, and loves it still.

In her first four years there were no playmates with whom she could share her comings and goings. She was very close to her parents, but not all that dependent upon them. Most working ranchers expect their children to assume responsibilities at an early age, and Sandra did not disappoint her parents.

She was given a gentle horse to ride as soon as her legs were long enough to reach the stirrups with the straps as short as they would go. Her father taught her how to sit straight in the saddle and the other basics of horseback riding. When he was too busy to ride with her, there was always a cowboy to watch her as she became more and more adventurous. She was soon allowed out of the smallest fenced pasture.

By the time Sandra was four her mother was teaching her to read by the mail-order Calvert method. Her lessons were delivered once a week by the postal service. It was a game she enjoyed, but her mother realized there was a limit to what she could offer her daughter. Sandra could learn to string letters together to recognize words, and she could sort out words to build a story, but there was no one of this same magical age with whom to read the story.

Ada Mae made the same decision Harry's father had made a generation before. This sort of education just wasn't good enough for a bright little girl whose curiosity was bound to expand beyond the borders of the ranch. Sandra would have to leave home to attend regular school. Grandmother and Grandfather Wilkey in El Paso were pleased to have a permanent visitor during the school year.

Sandra hated to leave the ranch, but she knew that there was no use arguing with her parents, and her grandmother would certainly not put up with any whining. She may have bitten her lip and been very solemn on the day of departure, but there were no tears. Her mother promised there would always be holidays at the ranch to look forward to, and on the weekends she and Sandra's father would come for a visit.

School brought many exciting new things into Sandra's world. There were set rules to be followed. A clock set the schedule for the day. At the ranch classes had started whenever Sandra's mother finished setting the kitchen to rights, and lessons could be broken if her father came in and suggested a ride to a far pasture.

As a "second" mother and father Sandra was very lucky to have such warm and understanding grandparents. Willis Wilkey was in poor health, but Grandmother Mamie was well able to handle the household, even with a new young boarder who would probably attract a string of playmates.

If there is anyone who might be considered a role model for Sandra, it is her grandmother, a self-sufficient woman who had come West in a covered wagon. She had seen her husband put down his roots and prosper. And more important, she had helped establish that success.

She was kind, but strict. A yardstick was used for the few times discipline was needed. Mamie Wilkey had not had a great deal of education herself, but she was an extremely intelligent woman who had seen to it that her own daughter, Sandra's mother, earned a college degree. There was no doubt that Sandra would be enrolled in the finest school available. Parents and grandmother selected Radford, an excellent private school in El Paso, which Sandra's

cousin Flournoy Davis attended. Flournoy's mother
and Sandra's mother were sisters. The girls were just
a year apart in age, and they were soon inseparable.
People began calling them the Davis-Day twins, although they were not look-alikes, for Flournoy had
long blond hair, and Sandra's was darker and curly.

There were other relatives too. Family gatherings
were frequent. Sandra had little chance to be lonely,
although there were times at night in her own room
when she began to count the days before the next
trip to the ranch.

Sandra Day O'Connor and her cousin Flournoy Davis were
junior bridesmaids at the 1937 wedding of Gates and Elizabeth
Davis.

She did have to admit that classes at school were more fun than lessons at the kitchen table. Once she set her mind to it, Sandra applied herself well, never requiring any urging to study. Flournoy was an equally good student, and the two girls used to enjoy reading books together. They also had a set of Dionne quintuplet dolls that were very much a part of their games.

Flournoy owned a bike. After school she would often pick up Sandra, who would perch on the seat behind her cousin. They would ride up and down the neighborhood visiting friends and relatives and stopping wherever there was something or someone of interest.

Flournoy remembers a favorite great aunt who wore a size two-and-a-half shoe. This was just right for two six-year-olds to slip into when playing "grown-up." In fact, fashion shows were often in order. Scarves, hats, and high-heeled shoes made for a dramatic day of play. "And here comes Miss Day wearing pink with a touch of purple." There would then be gales of laughter.

Jean Miller was a friend who joined the cousins in their one professional dramatic production. They selected a play, memorized the parts exactly, planned their costumes, and practiced stage makeup, borrowing from parents' and grandparents' supplies. Now who was going to come to see them perform?

Jean's father was in the printing business. He came to the rescue by printing up advertising fliers and tickets. The proceeds were to go to the milk fund for the needy.

It is not on record as to just how much that donation amounted to, but it gave the young cast a wonderful diversion for one entire month. They even oversold "the house," which happened to be the Miller garage.

In the summertime when vacation came, Flournoy would pack her suitcase and go off to the ranch with Sandra. The dolls came along, but there were exciting outdoor things to do, like learning to swim in the stock tank.

Here again Harry Day had been innovative and farsighted. He had experimented with installing steel-lined holding tanks to water the cattle, instead of the earth-banked reservoirs used in the past. Every spare drop of water from the sky was collected in these tanks, which stood some six feet above ground level. Windmills pumped water from deep wells when the sky was cloudless for months at a time. A few fish were put in the tanks to control the algae and keep the water clean. When a valve was opened water flushed into troughs for the animals to drink.

There was a big tank near the ranch house that served as a first-class swimming pool. Dotted over the entire ranch there were smaller tanks, so that any time a rider felt parched and ready for a dip, he or she had only to head for the horizon spiked by a windmill.

There was a shallow stream up toward the hills where the girls tried their hand at fishing. A branch was used for a pole and a safety pin for a hook. The catch was apt to be very small, but the girls had a wonderful time.

Cousin Flournoy remembers, "We played with dolls, but we knew what to do with screwdrivers and nails too. Living on a ranch made us very self-sufficient."

Several kinds of gourds grew wild on the ranch. When cut and cleaned they made beautiful tea sets for the children's pretend "tea parties."

There were always cowboys around who were kind and helpful. One year they made each of the girls a pair of stilts. And so another game was invented.

From the time she was eight, Sandra's father taught her to brand cattle, mend fences, and ride in roundups. "Bug" Quinn, who has been a hand at the Lazy B since 1918, remembered that she was not bad as a cowgirl. "She wasn't the rough and rugged type, but she worked well in the canyons. She held her own."

"There was plenty to do on that ranch," he continued. "When I was working fence I thought the place was as big as Texas. It took nearly 30 days to ride it."

Sandra's knowledge of those fences and how they were strung once saved her a lot of grief. Flournoy remembers on one of their expeditions they almost got lost. Both girls were good riders, and they were trusted on their own when they went exploring.

One day they had ridden as far as Cottonwood Canyon where the ancient Indians had carved their drawings on the sheer rock walls. It was a spooky place, supposedly haunted by the spirits of the past.

Sandra and Flournoy had taken longer than they had realized to climb the rocks and touch this long-ago recording of history. What had happened to these people? They talked about it and made guesses. Shadows began to cut across the canyon as the sun dipped lower on the horizon. They both agreed they'd better head for home, but which way was the direct route?

"I was scared," Flournoy recalled, "but Sandra always knew how to follow the fence lines. Different pastures were fenced different ways, but if you could follow the fence lines, eventually they would lead you back to the house.

"I guess we were regular rednecks, carrying twenty-twos everywhere we went," Flournoy continued. "Sandra and I were pretty good shots. Harry expected everybody to keep the critter population down by shooting jackrabbits, prairie dogs, coyotes, Gila monsters—anything that ate his pasture grass or went after the cattle."

They played a lot of card games too, and Sandra was a whiz. They read everything they could get their hands on. *The Wall Street Journal* was not exactly their favorite, although it was delivered regularly to the ranch, but the *National Geographic* and *The Saturday Evening Post* were read aloud from cover to cover.

Flournoy remembers that twice their literary tastes got them into trouble. "Once Sandra and I got into Ada Mae's love letters from Harry, and another time we talked a cowboy's wife into letting us read copies of *True Romance*."

Mrs. Day gave them an hour's lecture and curtailed their exploring for a while.

Sandra also learned to drive an old truck on the ranch at the early age of eight. That privilege was not to be used for joy rides but to help in the work on the ranch which she was expected to do during her vacation months. It was work she enjoyed.

"I didn't do all the things boys did," she says, "but I fixed windmills and repaired fences."

It took a certain amount of daring to climb a rickety ladder to set a windmill blade, but once up there it was like being on top of the world. There were a few rolling hills within the perimeter of the Lazy B, but nothing to stop the eye from looking as far away as forever, it seemed.

Such a view was impossible in the city. There,

land was blocked off in squares with streets and houses, and the silence was broken with traffic noise and the rush of people. Even the sky was different and the weather calmer.

Weather was always a topic of conversation. Harry Day always listened to the radio at news time to find out what was predicted. But the radio wasn't always reliable. Sometimes not even the faintest signal got through. When one day's heat piled onto another cloudless day, the soaring temperatures could interfere with reception.

Often a sudden change in the weather would surprise them. When the wind howled it seemed to pick up half the soil in Arizona. There was no driving through those banks of raw yellow clouds that hugged the land that the wind swept clean.

Lightning at the ranch was more spectacular than in the shelter of the city. You could see it come out of the vast sky and strike the ground. Sandra remembers hearing of her mother's close call. A blinding ball of lightning flashed through the kitchen window, struck the opposite wall, and finally dissipated its force with a sizzling crackle in the ground. The only thing that saved Mrs. Day was the fact she was bending over to put something in the oven.

4

Sandra hated to go back to El Paso in the fall. Her father remembers, "She'd always hide when it was time to return. Once she and Flournoy were swimming in the water tank and refused to come out. I got a lariat and roped them both out of the water. 'Back to school with you girls,' I said."

And back to school they went, sometimes by car, sometimes by train from the nearby stop at Lordsburg, New Mexico. Later a Greyhound bus connected that town with El Paso, but it was a long, rough trip with no superhighways to smooth the ride.

When Sandra was in third grade Grandfather Wilkey died. It was a sad time, of course, but Grandma took it in her stride, determined to care for the living and tend to their needs as she had always done. The family gathered round, and their strength added to hers.

Mamie Wilkey was not left alone, but those who

came to offer comfort soon found they were receiving more than they gave. Grandma had the right words to say to solve many a minor problem. Who else would they all turn to for advice and help?

Vacations now meant that Grandma often packed up and went to the ranch too. Most of the time things went smoothly, but Sandra's father remembers "her getting on me about letting Sandra ride in the rumble seat on top of a box of dynamite I was going to use to blast a new water tank."

It was not too unreasonable a complaint, but the ferocity of her lecture made it quite clear she wasn't sure whether the parents should ever be given the responsibility for their daughter again.

There was another big change around this time. Sandra's mother came back to El Paso for a while to have a baby, Sandra's sister Ann. Grandmother Mamie was busier than ever which pleased her no end. Two years later a brother named Alan was born.

Sandra was delighted and begged to have a chance to take care of them. She played with them as if she were a pretend mother.

Alan recalls with a grin, "She was a stern big sister to us though. When she said something we did it."

Sandra begged to join the family during the school year. She seemed so genuinely distressed she wasn't "part of the family" that Mr. and Mrs. Day decided, against their better judgment, to let her try the school in Lordsburg, some thirty miles from the ranch.

Transportation to and from school proved to be a real problem. "She had to be driven before dawn over to a homesteader's house to wait for the school bus," her father remembers. "If she took the bus home, it was after dark before she got here, so we'd try to have somebody drive over to Lordsburg to pick her up. She still had a long wait after classes, which didn't give her all that much time to enjoy the ranch or the kids."

Sandra settled down to apply herself to a different school curriculum and a different set of friends. She was considered an outsider, only because the other students had all been together since first grade.

The majority of Sandra's classmates spoke Spanish as their first language, but it is a credit to her excellent scholarship that Sandra had the highest grade in that subject of anyone in the class. Ada Mae made sure that there was plenty of studying at home to make up for the limited curriculum at Lordsburg.

Sandra had gotten her wish to be home, but somehow she missed all the Wilkey relatives and the friends she had made in El Paso. It didn't take too much persuading to get her to return to Radford, especially when she had read some of Flournoy's letters.

Toward the very end of the year she returned to the Radford School in El Paso. After consultation with the teaching staff it was decided that she should skip a grade. She had already passed her friends in many of the subjects.

She'd grown up too. "That year she stayed home was the year she lost her little girl appearance," Cita Schuster, a Radford school friend recalls. "I saw her at the end of the summer at a birthday party. Suddenly she was so tall and tan and so pretty in a white dress, while I still had my baby fat."

Cita was often invited to the ranch. "Some of the happiest times I can remember were at the Lazy B," she says. "I liked everything about it, especially her daddy. He had the brightest eyes and—I don't know— you just knew he was 'somebody.' Some mornings we'd get up early and go on the ranch with him, but we had to be quiet and behave ourselves."

Sandra's mother was an excellent cook and she loved to entertain. Although in the early years of their marriage the Days lived quite an isolated life, in later years it wasn't all that unusual for her to be preparing food for a hundred or so. She made sure that Sandra was capable in the kitchen and knew how to organize the preparation of a meal.

Hondey Hill McAllister says, "She (Sandra's mother) taught me how to make black-bottom pie one summer, and I still make it, although it takes half a day. I think Sandra cooked family meals once a week."

Although the ranch was isolated, Sandra's parents were very concerned with the world outside the Lazy B. Politics were rarely discussed, although Harry had eventually become a registered Republican in the overwhelmingly Democratic county of Greenlee, mostly to discourage his friends, he remembers gleefully, from pushing him into running for something.

To give his family a little clearer idea of what the rest of the world was like, one summer he packed them into the car and drove them to every state capital west of the Mississippi.

"And we climbed to the dome of every capitol," Alan recalls, "until finally we had to come home." That trip took the complete summer.

There were other trips too, including fishing trips in the Gulf of Mexico. Harry Day often returned to California where he had spent his own boyhood. Balboa Island was a favorite place to visit. Swimming in the ocean was very different from swimming in a stock tank. It was exciting, and the broad expanse of water was vast like the rolling empty range land.

When Flournoy's family spent time at their cabin in the mountains near Cloudcroft, New Mexico, Sandra and Grandmother Wilkey almost always went along.

Sandra's horizons had already stretched beyond the Lazy B.

5

After one last year at Radford, Sandra entered Austin High School in El Paso. She was twelve years old. Her former teachers remember her as a very capable and well-rounded girl.

"Some might have thought she was a little shy, but I think she was just mature and reserved," said Mrs. Chaffee, who taught her history. "She was always perfectly groomed, and there was a hint of elegance about her." This was a trait she probably learned or inherited from her mother.

Her close friends never considered her shy. Hondey says, "Sandra always knew how to handle herself. She was in honor classes and was terrific at impromptu speaking, but she also did all the normal things teenagers did—had crushes and talked about boys. She was just never loud or awkward. I wasn't jealous of her, but I remember feeling a little inferior. She could really do everything well."

Those compliments have followed her all through her life. Sandra modestly turns them aside. She credits her life at the ranch for much of this aura of self-assurance and confidence. "You were just expected to do your part. Nobody received praise for doing a job. In ranching you learn to make do. We couldn't always be running to a store when something broke. You were trained for all emergencies."

Still, not every young person raised on a ranch has such an impressive record of accomplishments. What made the difference? Sandra was a bright self-starter of enormous energy who never needed to be coaxed to do a job well. She had an extra amount of brilliance that made her very special.

She was sixteen when she graduated from high school. She applied to only one college, Stanford. That had been her father's choice before his father's death had canceled his own plans for college, but it was Sandra's very own independent decision. She liked the West, and besides, this was one of the finest universities in the country.

She thought first of becoming a geologist. She enjoyed science. With all the oil and mineral wealth still to be discovered in the country around her, it seemed like a fine choice. And she loved the out-of-doors so much. Perhaps this work would keep her outside an office part of the time.

It was a question either of becoming a geologist or

Sandra Day O'Connor as a sophomore at Stanford University.

of returning to her first love, ranching. She enjoyed photography as a hobby, and her subject matter was the beauty of nature. She still has a very fine collection.

She doesn't remember what steered her toward law. Certainly if she were to take an interest in the running of the ranch, which she hoped to share with her sister and brother, a knowledge of law would be helpful. And it was this that may have influenced her choice.

Once the decision was made, she focused all her energy upon it. She signed up for the maximum permitted courses each semester, several times having to get special approval for an overload.

Marilyn Brown, her sophomore roommate, remembers her as a rather quiet young woman with the soft accents of western speech who seemed more than equal to university life.

"Even though she was younger than us (her classmates), she always seemed to handle it. She never got upset. She never went into a panic about anything. She was easy to get along with and she was fun."

Sandra saved time for her friends. She was never considered a "grind." Absolute self-discipline and organization of time is the only accountable explanation for all she was able to accomplish during her college days and beyond. Her trips back to the ranch were only for short spells to regenerate her energy.

"She used to bring a bunch of girls from Stanford for the spring roundup," her father remembers, "and I'd tell her, 'Sandra, I don't have time to be saddling horses for a bunch of sissies,' but you know, those kids just took care of themselves pretty well."

When the short vacations were over it was back to the books. She registered for summer semesters as well, planning on graduating with her law degree in six years instead of the usual seven. Her bachelor's degree was in economics.

Her ability was recognized by teachers and students alike. She was elected to the prestigious honorary society Order of the Coif, which accepts only the very best law students. She won a post on the *Stanford Law Review*, where she met her future husband, another bright young law student. He was one class behind Sandra but shared several classes with her. His name was John Jay O'Connor III.

They had dinner the first night they met while working on the *Law Review*. It was the first of forty-six straight dates. From then on everyone else was excluded from both their social calendars.

The Days knew John was a very special guest the first time Sandra brought him back to the Lazy B. She took great pains to show him around, to try to have him understand why she loved this bleak part of the world so much.

John came from an old San Francisco family which

had made a considerable fortune as the frontier town grew into a cosmopolitan city. His father was a prominent doctor. John knew little about ranching, but on this first weekend visit he was learning.

"We liked him," Harry remembers with a grin, "but I've seen better cowboys."

Ada Mae reminded him that if Sandra had been looking for a cowboy she probably wouldn't have headed for Stanford.

Sandra graduated magna cum laude with highest honors, ranking third in a class of 102 graduates. William Rehnquist, who would later be her colleague on the Supreme Court, was first.

John still had one more year before he could take the bar exam, but he and Sandra decided to get married before then. The bride and groom were both twenty-two. The date was set for December 20, 1952. Arrangements were made to have the ceremony at the ranch. A large brand-new barn had just been built, and it was beautifully decorated for the occasion.

Although the Days had not been regular churchgoers, more because of distance to the nearest town than lack of religious beliefs, they were Episcopalians. John Jay O'Connor had been brought up in the Catholic church, but neither then nor now has religion been an issue of disagreement between the O'Connors. Both families were pleased with their new in-laws, and a big celebration was planned.

More than two hundred guests arrived, the Governor of New Mexico among them. Every guest room was full, and the one motel within commuting distance was filled. Some guests brought their campers, younger ones brought their sleeping bags.

It all went to create a very warm feeling for Sandra, with friends and family gathered together in the one place in the world she loved the most. Yet she was not afraid of the future away from the ranch. It would always be there to come back to.

John returned to school. Sandra went job hunting. She suddenly collided head-on with the legal profession's prejudice against women.

"I interviewed with law firms in Los Angeles and San Francisco," she says, "but none had ever hired a woman before as a lawyer, and they were not prepared to do so."

One of the firms to which she applied was Gibson, Dunn and Crutcher in Los Angeles, and one of the partners was William French Smith. Later, as Attorney General of the United States he would be recommending her for the highest position the law has to offer. At this time the firm was only prepared to offer her a job as a legal secretary.

She had no intention of letting her diploma collect dust unused. So instead she decided to try government service. In 1952 she started her first job as a deputy county attorney in San Mateo, California. It

Sandra Day and John O'Connor hold their son Scott at his Baptism in Phoenix in 1957. *—Phoenix Newspapers, Inc.*

was fine experience and she still had time to be with John.

When later asked how this early rejection by the legal establishment may have affected her feelings about women's rights, she insisted in her calm and steady way that she was not bitter. "I wasn't frustrated," she said. "I just redirected toward public service, and it hasn't been disappointing."

The draft was in force, and when John graduated he joined the army's Judge Advocate General's Corps and was sent to Frankfurt, West Germany. Sandra went with him.

Never one to sit around and waste time, Sandra worked as a civilian lawyer for the Quartermaster Corps. She and John took advantage of what free time they had together to travel through Europe. They toured museums and churches and explored the fabulous capitals of Europe, but what they enjoyed most of all were the mountains that so often surrounded them. It was here in the Alps that they both first fell in love with skiing. It took only a few lessons before they were tackling some of the very steep runs. It is a sport they've continued to enjoy and have taught their three sons to enjoy.

6

Now the transient phase of their lives was over. It was time to put down roots. In 1957 they settled in Phoenix, Arizona, still less than a day's drive to the ranch. John was hired by a fine law firm, Fennemore, Craig, von Ammon & Udall, and they started looking around for a house to buy. Nothing quite suited them.

As John explained it, "It was to be our first home. We wanted it to be a masterpiece within our means."

They wisely chose to buy a large piece of property which would lend itself to expansion and additions as their incomes and needs increased. From the beginning Sandra had shared her enthusiasm with John for the type of architecture indigenous to the Southwest. What could be better than adobe, the native building material?

The first structure on the site covered a modest 1800 square feet, built almost entirely by hand in

1958. Their friends more than once were surprised to find them both in overalls soaking each adobe brick in coat after coat of milk.

"It's supposed to give the clay a certain sheen," Sandra explained. "It's an old technique, but I don't know why you use skim and not homogenized milk."

Over the years their house in Paradise Valley, a suburb of Phoenix, has spread in all directions. A sweeping roof overhang protects their adobe walls from rain. There is a pool and a guest house now, but the simple earthen building material echoes the owners' love of the earth and the historic beginnings of the first native Americans who lived in these same desert surroundings.

Sandra set up her own private practice for a while. It included every conceivable type of law, everything from leases to drunken-driving cases. She was hard-working and thorough no matter how small the case.

Raising a family of their own was definitely on the O'Connor schedule of events. For five years Sandra says she retired to have children, but other members of her family remember that along with being a very conscientious mother, she was always busy with some type of professional activity.

First came Scott, two years later came Brian, and two years after Brian their youngest son Jay was born. Never once did she mention to anyone that she missed her career, but there were times when she must have had questions about her future.

Sharon Percy Rockefeller, a close friend since they served on the Board of Trustees of Stanford University, says, "Sandra is clearly a role model for younger women. She understands very well the conflict between a woman's desires to be part of the professional world and yet to be a perfect mother as well. Sandra is serenity itself. If anyone was born to be a judge, Sandra was."

Even during those early years Sandra was able to juggle a very busy schedule and not seem to be harried or rushed.

"The O'Connors have a very happy marriage, and he's real proud of her," says Virginia Hash, a Phoenix attorney. "Though they've had a housekeeper, Sandra is a gourmet cook. She's even entered cooking contests. I know her to be a warm, loving mother who enjoys playing tennis and swimming with her family. She's got a great sense of humor and fun, but her best trait is that she never gets mad in an argument."

John O'Connor agrees. "You look at her resume, and you think, 'My God, the woman must be some kind of machine,' but the amazing thing is that she has always retained her priorities. The family always came first."

It must be said that Sandra O'Connor has a very supportive and encouraging husband, secure in his own career. Sharing the same profession has given each of them an understanding of the problems and pressures of their working day.

During her days of "retirement" Sandra lent her talents to many volunteer organizations. She served as adviser to the Salvation Army, she was an auxiliary volunteer at a school for blacks and Hispanics, and she was elected president of the Phoenix Junior League.

Mrs. Betsy Taylor, who preceded her as president of the League and has been an extremely close friend of the family, repeats what many have said, "She knows how to organize her time. She never wastes a minute, but she never gives the impression of being rushed. She's always gracious."

John O'Connor more than kept pace with Sandra on volunteer boards. He has chaired the Arizona Crippled Children's Services, the United Way, Mental Health Association, and Legal Aid Society. The list goes on and on. He has been on the board of two hospitals and active in the Young Republicans. It has been pointed out that John O'Connor was listed in *Who's Who* before his now famous wife.

The O'Connors enjoyed an active social life. John is a very outgoing person with a wonderful sense of humor. He is an excellent speaker and was often asked to be master of ceremonies at affairs in Phoenix. He loves to entertain guests with Irish jokes told in a brogue.

As a couple the O'Connors could have accepted invitations for almost every day of the year. Here is where they both set priorities. Many of their plans included the boys and their friends, but time was also set aside to sit at home and enjoy each other.

When they did go out it was never a duty affair, they sincerely enjoyed it. Stanford vice-president Joel Smith recalls her as "the best dancer I've ever danced with. She also enjoys country music."

Sandra has always loved sports. She set her mind to learning to play golf in the same way she applied herself to more serious matters. Even though she hasn't had the time to play as often as she would like, she is a good competitive golfer with an eighteen handicap. Many full-time golfers would value that record.

And there was always the ranch. Frequently on weekends they would all pile into the family car and head for the gentle rolling hills of the Lazy B. As their sons got older they learned to ride and rope from foreman Cole Webb, and the ranch was where most of their summers were spent.

Told that if anything ever happened to his parents he could live on the ranch for the rest of his life, Jay O'Connor, then eight, saved up the ten-dollar bus fare he would need to get there. He kept it stashed away for months, just in case. The boys still consider the ranch their second home.

Although the Days will never admit there is a

favorite in their family, there is certainly a flash of pride that beams brightly whenever they talk about their oldest child.

Ada Mae sees a humility in Sandra, explaining, "She isn't the type who would try to high-hat anyone."

She gives as an example Sandra's patience one day when she was trying to run an errand for Scott. Sandra was president of the Hoard Indian Museum, which holds an annual handicraft sale. There was an item Scott wanted very much, but he couldn't go himself because he had just broken his leg in a skiing accident. There were lines of people waiting to get in. Instead of using her clout to bypass the other buyers, Sandra spent several hours sitting on a camp stool to await her turn.

Behavior like this is just another reason why she is respected.

7

In 1965, about the time her youngest son entered school, Sandra chose to continue her law career on a full-time basis. "Finally I decided I needed a paid job so that my life would be more orderly," she recalls.

She spent four years as an assistant attorney general in Arizona. It was a satisfying job and a fulfilling one. Almost as many hours a day had been given to volunteer work, but without a specific commitment her life had seemed less organized. And an organized life is what Sandra requires to be happy.

She had discovered this her very first day in school. Classes at the kitchen table at home had been fun and relaxed, but to feel she was really accomplishing something, a clock had to tick off a schedule.

In 1969 Sandra O'Connor was appointed by the Maricopa County Board of Supervisors to fill a vacancy as a state senator. She had been asked before to run for any number of political posts, but she had never looked forward to the campaigning. Actually Sandra was too modest to be a good campaigner. She felt her record should stand for itself without a lot of speech making.

But on this occasion she was able to bypass this part of politics. She accepted the appointment and set about her job with enthusiasm.

Sandra was active in framing several pieces of important legislation. Alice Bendheim, a Phoenix attorney, recalls one instance.

"I first met her in 1969 when I was in law school. I had written a comment in the law journal on community property. In those days, only the husband could manage and control community property [in the state of Arizona].

"A reporter picked up my article, and O'Connor asked a mutual friend to have me call. When I did, she said, 'Why don't you come down to the legislature and help me change the community property law?'

"The following fall, she got together a committee of legislators, lawyers, business people, and women's rights people, and we rewrote the law and she got it through. She made it a noncontroversial bill—a part of the marriage and divorce law—and she shepherded it through the senate in a very shrewd way. It passed without fanfare, which is the only way it could have passed."

There has been much talk about her stand on ERA

(the Equal Rights Amendment). Sandra voted for ratification of the amendment in the Arizona legislature, but it was said she wasn't a strong supporter of it. Several more active leaders in the fight wanted to bring it out of committee to find out where people stood. O'Connor didn't want a floor vote because she was afraid the opposition would then be able to cancel any gains the measure's supporters had been able to make. However, she chaired the committee that revised several Arizona statutes that discriminated against women in areas such as the number of hours they were permitted to work, parental consent, and child-custody matters.

Shirley Odegard says, "Although Sandra O'Connor was not a part of the women's movement, she's been supportive of women's issues without being on the stump and marching in demonstrations."

Susan Freeman, another lawyer, describes her as "concerned about women and about people generally, but she's certainly not a radical feminist."

Her devotion to detail soon became legendary. She once offered an amendment to a bill merely to insert a missing, but important, comma.

The next year she ran successfully on her own and was elected to a two-year term of office as a state senator, and by 1972 her seventeen admiring Republican colleagues elected her majority leader of the Arizona State Senate. She was the first woman to

In 1972 Sandra Day O'Connor and John Van Huegel were named Phoenix Woman and Man of the Year.

—*Phoenix Newspapers, Inc.*

serve as majority leader of any state senate in the nation. She won the post because of general respect for her intelligence and her insistence on precision rather than on "political savvy popularity." It was a case, as one person put it, of "talent winning out."

"She does not have charisma, in the sense of stirring speeches, that kind of thing," said Bill Jacquin, who was president of the Arizona State Senate in the early seventies, "but she does have the abillty to make an articulate speech that is founded on facl and that's what I was looking for."

Her legislative achievements ranged from tax relief, which included support of measures to limit state spending, to flood control funding. During her terms of office the death penalty was restored in the state of Arizona. She was in favor of strict crime preventive measures but equally concerned with prison reforms.

Democratic State Senator Alfred Gutierrez says, "She worked interminable hours and read everything there was. It was impossible to win a debate with her. We'd go on the floor with a few facts and let rhetoric do the rest. Not Sandra. She would overwhelm you with her knowledge."

As majority leader, she learned both tact and toughness. One committee chairman was furious at what he considered O'Connor's failure to finish up the senate's business by the time of adjournment.

Red in the face and fuming, he shouted, "If you were a man I'd punch you in the mouth."

She snapped right back, "If you were a man you could."

It was perhaps the need for this kind of toughness that tarnished her bright enthusiasm for politics. Her senate colleague Anne Lindeman said, "She was more comfortable with law. Because she is so intense, she really doesn't suffer fools gladly, and in the legislature you have to suffer fools constantly."

Yet it surprised everyone that she did not seek re-election to the state senate. Instead, she ran for and won a spot on the Maricopa Superior Court in 1974.

As a trial judge Sandra was stern but fair. One of her early cases involved a Scottsdale mother of two infants who pleaded guilty to passing bad checks totaling $3500. She begged mercy of the court claiming the children would become wards of the state.

O'Connor sentenced the woman to five to ten years in prison, saying, "You should have known better." But when she got back to her chambers she admitted she broke down in tears. This was not the woman's first offense, and this stern punishment seemed the only way to turn her life around.

Burton Barr, Arizona House majority leader says, "She's not going to coddle the criminal. Her decisions as a Superior Court judge were tough. If you have done something wrong you are going to pay."

Another associate reports that O'Connor had strong interests in prison conditions. "She was known as a stiff sentencer, but she is also concerned about what happens to the guy once he's in the can." She feels that more one-to-one counseling should be available in prison.

A less well-known episode involves her presiding at a trial of a battered wife who shot her husband. The woman was found guilty despite her plea of self-defense. Judge O'Connor was angry with the defense attorney. She told him that she thought the woman would not have been convicted if he had presented the case properly. She imposed the minimum sentence provided by law and supported the woman's request for a commutation of her sentence.

At least twice she advised defendants to get new attorneys because their lawyers were unprepared. The law was there for their protection as well as to provide for their prosecution.

Judge O'Connor did not hesitate to order the death penalty for Mark Koch, who had been found guilty of hiring himself out as a killer. His victim was involved in the sale of drugs. Again it was a hard decision, but one she was prepared to make.

She was once referred to in the press as the "Dragon Lady," but in personal terms, Sandra Day O'Connor is someone almost everyone likes. She has often been described as cold or austere, but also as fair, nice, and with an ideal family life.

Sharon Percy Rockefeller, who knows her well, says that once you are close to her that austere facade disappears. "Sandra O'Connor brings to her job extreme personal dignity. Her life is lived according to a set of what some might call old-fashioned manners. She is extremely considerate of others."

At one time she was tempted to run for the United States Senate, but the fact she would be opposing Barry Goldwater, a friend, made her dismiss those plans immediately. It would be only courteous to wait for another time.

She is sincerely interested in other people. Sharon Rockefeller pictures her as a warm, kind, outgoing friend. "She almost always starts a conversation by asking how my family is. It is not a perfunctory kind of question. She really does want to know. She cares."

About this time in the mid-70s Republican leaders in Arizona were urging her to run for governor against the incumbent Democrat, Bruce Babbitt. She declined, and just eleven months later Governor Babbitt nominated her to the Court of Appeals. There were some politicians who said Babbitt was simply trying to eliminate his competition.

Babbitt insists, "I had to find the finest talent available to create confidence in our new merit system. Her intellectual ability and her judgment are astounding."

Sandra Day O'Connor takes the oath of office as Maricopa County Superior Court Judge in 1975.

—Phoenix Newspapers, Inc.

What he said was true, but he'd found an excellent way to keep that intellectual ability from opposing him.

Sandra's statement was that she preferred the law to being head of the state government. She summed up her love for the law by saying, "It's marvelous because it is always changing."

She never voiced disappointment that she did not continue her studies in geology, and although she doesn't have much time for riding the range, she has found a very satisfying life.

She's never lost touch with the Lazy B. She is still one of the owners of the ranch, although her brother Alan has taken over the active management. He smiles when he adds, "Yes, and she questions every penny I spend."

Harry Day had finally gotten his wish to have some firsthand legal advisors in the family, but he jokingly complains about his daughter's diligence.

"She's so damned conscientious," he says, "she wouldn't even give me a legal opinion. As a judge she can't, so she refers me to her husband."

On the appeals court she didn't face any landmark cases, but she did manage to cut the court's caseload by persuading her former colleagues in the senate to clarify laws involving workmen's compensation and unemployment compensation. Cases involving these complaints had been piling up on the court docket beyond reasonable numbers. Other types of cases consisted largely of appeals from criminal convictions, divorces, and bankruptcies.

Generally she upheld trial judges. The appeals court never hears a case that hasn't already been judged by a lower court. In an article she wrote for the *William and Mary Law Review*, she urged federal judges to give greater weight to the findings of state courts. She reasoned that when a state judge moves up to a federal bench, "he does not become immediately better equipped intellectually to do a job."

A Justice Department official says approvingly, "She was not leaping out to overrule trial court judges or state lawyers to craft novel theories. Her opinions are sensible and scholarly."

"What her opinions do show," said another, "is a careful study of precedent, ample citation, and a clear no-nonsense writing style that some of the justices of the Supreme Court might do well to emulate."

8

One job after another was bringing Sandra Day
O'Connor critical acclaim in her own state, but few
outside of Arizona had heard her name. From an
intermediate court of appeals to United States Supreme Court justice is quite a step. Just how did
Sandra happen to be chosen for this position?

The first step was a campaign promise by Presi-
dential candidate Ronald Reagan pledging that a
woman would fill "one of the first vacancies on the
Supreme Court in my administration."

Barely four months into Reagan's term, Justice
Potter Stewart told Attorney General William French
Smith that he intended to resign during the summer
of 1981. Smith began collecting names of possible
replacements. By May his aides had full files on at
least two dozen candidates. White House counsel
Fred Fielding had drawn up a similar list.

Both lists gave the President three categories of

choices: prominent conservative lawyers, old friends like top aide Edwin Meese III, and a list of prominent women lawyers and judges.

The President said he wanted to be sure that the most capable candidate was nominated regardless of sex. He knew he would be criticized if the candidate for such a high post, whether male or female, was not qualified.

But O'Connor's name turned up on all lists, and she had powerful friends. She had known Chief Justice Burger for some time and had recently renewed their friendship at a meeting of Anglo-American lawyers. She was also, of course, a former classmate of another justice of the Supreme Court, William H. Rehnquist.

On June 18, 1981, Potter Stewart formally announced his resignation after nearly twenty-three years of service. It was hoped that a replacement could be approved in time for that person to participate in the fall Court hearings. Much had to take place in the meantime.

On June 23, 1981, Smith sent a Justice Department lawyer to Phoenix to gather additional information on O'Connor. He had several conversations with her on the phone. Four days later two other government lawyers flew to Arizona and spent the day at the O'Connor home.

Heady technical discussions concerning the philosophies of federal and state responsibility in the courts were interrupted when the judge went to see about the serving of a luncheon she had prepared herself.

In the meantime a team of FBI investigators spent two weeks providing their detailed report. In addition, both Republican and Democratic House and Senate staffers asked their own questions, and Sandra had to clear her calendar for more interviews.

One reporter breezed into her office and found her usually tidy desk cluttered with papers. Her husband and her law clerk were sorting through files trying to help with the review. Judge O'Connor looked up with a sigh, "It's a nightmare. Fifty years is a long time, and it's hard to remember everything you did."

Dozens of people were interviewed. Every vote she had cast as a legislator, every decision she had made as a judge was scrutinized carefully.

What they learned was that as a state and appellate judge, she was known as a serious student of the law who liked to keep her courtroom running smoothly. She displayed little patience with unprepared lawyers.

"She's pretty much known as an iron lady," said one Phoenix lawyer who recalled that Judge O'Connor "jumped on me with both feet" when he fumbled in trying to answer some of her questions during a trial. "In terms of her ability," he added, "she is a very bright lady. She knows a lot of law."

"She's far from a shrinking violet," said Donald F. Froeb, a colleague on the Arizona appeals court.

"She always assumes the intellectual leadership in a group discussion."

Sharon Rockefeller, who had observed her at many Stanford University Board of Trustees meetings, explained how she would listen to the issue being discussed, usually not offering any comments until everyone else had spoken. Then very slowly, thoughtfully she would outline the problem and offer a solution modestly without fanfare or histrionics. She never evaded issues by giving shadowy answers. If there was no immediate solution, her evaluation of the problem made the point clear.

Former Ambassador William F. Mahoney, another Phoenix lawyer, called Sandra O'Connor "fair, objective, and open minded. She runs a tight court. You get the feeling she's all business. She's not a winger," Mahoney added, "left or right."

Although other candidates were also undergoing close scrutiny, support for Sandra was building. Senator Barry Goldwater added his praise.

In the end Sandra was the only candidate asked to come to Washington for final talks. She flew to the capital on June 29, 1981, and met with Smith and his top aides, Ed Schmults and William Clark.

After passing that test, top members of the White House staff took over the questioning. Edwin Meese was accompanied by James Baker, Michael Deaver, and Fred Fielding. They met Sandra at the L'Enfant

In 1972 Sandra Day O'Connor participated in a debate on the floor of the Arizona State Senate.

Plaza Hotel in Washington, and for ninety minutes submitted one question after the other.

As one participant put it, "We were testing her psychological and intellectual stamina."

The next day when she met with Reagan the talk was mostly social. Then it was back home to Phoenix and an agonizing wait.

The final news came from two sources. First she had a call from her friend Warren Burger. It started out as a chatty talk, then moments after the conversation started she was forced to put the Chief Justice on hold while she accepted a call from the President of the United States. His message was that she had been selected to fill the vacancy on the Supreme Court. Would she accept?

Her answer was yes, but of course everything depended on the Senate Judiciary Committee approval and a vote of the U.S. Senate.

In the meantime President Reagan announced to the press that he had chosen "truly a person for all seasons, a woman who meets the very high standards that I demand of all Court appointees."

Sandra met with reporters in Phoenix on July 7, 1981. She said she "was extremely honored and happy" to be named to the Court. If confirmed, she promised to do her best "to serve the Court and the nation in a manner that will bring credit to the President, my family and the American people."

Feminist groups praised the nomination, if not the President who made it. The irony of the appointment was that it was made by a conservative president, whom the majority of women had voted against. Actually the women's movement, created in the early 1970s by radicals who came out of the civil rights movement and the New Left, had prepared the way for this woman, who was now being described as a "comfortable Republican conservative."

The criticism of the appointment came from the very people who would have been expected to support her, the New Right. Their complaints? They felt she was in favor of legalizing abortion, and they quoted from her record that she had supported the Equal Rights Amendment.

Some were concerned that she lacked experience in a federal court. These opponents were few in number but very loud in their protests. With this much vocal opposition, many people were afraid the President might withdraw his nomination.

It was not to be the case. It was up to the hearings in committee. These were to start on September 9, 1981. This was a long summer for Sandra Day O'Connor.

9

The atmosphere on the opening day of the hearings was warm and friendly. Honored guests were ushered into a large reserved area behind the witness table. O'Connor came down the aisle of the packed hearing room on the arm of Committee Chairman Senator Strom Thurmond. Both smiled to friends in the crowd.

Members of the audience stood to get a better look at this woman in the news, and several committee members rushed up like proud relatives to shake her hand and offer congratulations.

In her opening statement, Sandra pointedly introduced her husband and three sons who sat in the first row behind her, and then paid tribute to the "importance of families in our lives." She called marriage "the hope of the world and the strength of our country."

One reporter wrote, "She proved herself a lady

with traditional values that should be a shining example to a younger generation of women."

She made it clear from the beginning that she would not discuss issues that she might have to rule on at some future date. "I do not believe that, as a nominee, I can tell you how I might vote on a particular issue which may come before the Court, or endorse or criticize specific Supreme Court decisions presenting issues which may well come before the court again. To do so would mean that I have prejudiced the matter or have morally committed myself to a certain position. Such a statement by me as to how I might resolve a particular issue or what I might do in a future court action might make it necessary for me to disqualify myself."

She spoke slowly, measuring her words carefully. She sat in the witness chair erect, sometimes leaning forward toward the table in front of her to make a point. Gracefully but firmly folded hands were the only sign of nervousness. Drawing careful distinctions between personal views and any possible legal applications, she declined to answer about two dozen questions.

When asked to discuss her private meeting with the President in July, she firmly refused. "I should not properly reveal the contents of that conversation. It was not his request; that is my perception of what is proper."

The tone of the hearings changed on September 11, 1981, when several spokespersons for antiabortion groups testified against her nomination. "Right-to-Lifers" marched outside the Senate office building, carrying signs and shouting defiance. It was not easy for Sandra to see such displays of protest.

What apparently upset these ultraconservatives was not O'Connor's work as a state trial and appeals court judge, but votes she had cast as an Arizona legislator.

They pointed to three instances. First, in 1970 in a party caucus meeting she had favored a bill to make abortion legal. Second, she had voted against a resolution calling on Congress to pass an antiabortion constitutional amendment, feeling it was not an issue for legislation. And thirdly, in 1974 she cast a vote against a rider to a football stadium bond issue that would have barred abortions at the University of Arizona Hospital. Her vote was made on the grounds that the issue had nothing whatsoever to do with the bill on hand.

When questioned about her current stand on the issue, she said that she found "abortion personally abhorrent. My own view is that I am opposed to abortion either as birth control or otherwise," but she added, "I'm over the hill. I'm not going to be pregnant any more, so perhaps it is easy for me to draw such a strict line."

Sandra Day O'Connor at her desk after her nomination to the
U.S. Supreme Court. The jelly beans were a gift from a well-
wisher.   —*Wide World Photos*

In any case she emphasized that it was not a question for the courts to decide.

Those who supported her tried to get the Committee to look at her record as a whole. Joseph R.
Biden Jr., ranking Democrat on the Judiciary Committee countered, "It troubles me that we would re-
quire of a judge something beyond a profound sense
of the law."

Barry Goldwater said, "I don't buy the idea that
a justice of the Supreme Court has to stand for this
or that and the other thing."

O'Connor pointed out that she had supported one
bill restricting the use of Arizona state funds for

abortions and a second bill that gave hospital personnel the right not to participate in abortions.

Thad Cochran of Mississippi noted, "One thing this proves is that you can't please everybody."

"The real question is," said Howard M. Metzenbaum, "is this woman qualified? This committee will not be prevailed upon to make a decision on any single issue. The greatest threat or danger to representational democracy—the agreement to vote a certain way—can never be the price to be appointed to the federal court or confirmed by the Senate.

Senators asked her how she perceived the role of judge in making social policy through judicial decisions. O'Connor answered that she believed it was proper for the judiciary only to interpret the Constitution and laws made by the legislature, not to make the laws—it was important for judges to rule on the facts before them and the relevant existing statutes or cases and not try to mirror changing values.

"I do not believe it is the function of the court to step in because times have changed or the social mores have changed."

She continued, "Judges are not only not authorized to engage in executive or legislative functions, they are also ill equipped to do so. Judges who purport to decide matters of public policy are certainly not as attuned to the public will as are members of the politically accountable branches.

"I do well understand the difference between legislating and judging. As a judge it is not my function to develop public policy."

State and local officials noted with enthusiasm that she is likely to help stop what Democratic Governor Bruce Babbitt of Arizona called "the erosion of our federal system" by curbing extensions of federal power at the expense of the states.

"After all," observed Committee Chairman Strom Thurmond, "O'Connor is the first Supreme Court nominee in 42 years with experience in a state legislature, the first in 24 years to come from a state court bench."

"She's from 'Sagebrush Rebellion country,' " said one Administrative official. "When they talk about states' rights out there, they mean it."

Sandra O'Connor had already laid down her principle, "I believe in the importance of the limited role of government generally and in the constitutional restraints on the judiciary in particular."

There were other questions too. Senator Edward Kennedy asked whether she had ever been the victim of sex bias. She noted that she had been unable to find a job in a private law firm after graduating from law school. "Employment discrimination against women has always been a matter of concern to me," she said. "There does seem to be a wide disparity in the earnings of women compared to men. Some divorce laws and other statutes treat women unfairly."

She reminded him that as an Arizona legislator she led successful efforts to repeal statutes that barred women from managing the community property of a married couple. She also said she believed in "vigorous enforcement" of civil rights laws.

Concerning busing, Sandra remembered the year she sometimes rode buses seventy-five miles a day to attend school in Lordsburg. She said that busing can be "disruptive" and "not terribly beneficial to the child." She did not say, however, how she would vote on specific school desegregation cases.

She said she favored capital punishment and the admission of relevant evidence obtained by police officers who were unaware they had made an unconstitutional search. And she advocated some form of preventive detention for suspects before trial when they are considered dangerous.

"The public is very, very distressed with the extent of crime in this country." She indicated she might favor tighter bail laws to make it more difficult for those with criminal records to be freed pending trial on new charges.

She acknowledged that a Supreme Court doctrine known as the exclusionary rule, which bars evidence obtained improperly from being submitted in trials, "has caused general public discontent."

Sandra Day O'Connor makes a point during confirmation hearings on her nomination to the U.S. Supreme Court.

—Wide World Photos

At the same time, however, she made it clear that these were personal views only. So there is a great risk in predicting how an appointee in a lifetime federal court job will vote.

During eleven hours in the witness chair she did not hesitate to politely challenge misstatements by lawmakers. At the same time she was painstakingly patient with senators who asked repetitious questions.

Sandra O'Connor's deft fielding of questions from the eighteen male politicians on the Senate panel suggested that she would have no problem holding her own in deliberations on the Supreme Court.

At the end her integrity remained unchallenged, her competence admired, her composure unruffled. Only one or two conservative senators, whose specific queries she had sidestepped, seemed unnerved by the experience.

On September 15, 1981, the final vote of the Committee was cast. Sandra Day O'Connor was approved 17-0 with Jeremiah Denton, the Republican from Alabama, abstaining. Denton's lack of confidence came because of O'Connor's refusal to discuss antiabortion legislation.

There was one more test to follow, perhaps the most important of all, approval by the one hundred members of the United States Senate.

10

The debate in the Senate was half-hearted. O'Connor's opponents knew they were fighting a losing battle, but as Sandra waited for the five-minute buzzer summoning the senators for the final balloting, she was obviously nervous. "This is the longest five minutes of my life," she said with an anxious smile.

The smile soon turned to a broad, but modest, grin of delight. By a vote of 99 to 0 the Senate made Judge Sandra Day O'Connor, Justice O'Connor, the first woman to serve on the Supreme Court of the United States. In its 191-year history, 101 justices have served on the nation's highest court.

The vote would have been a perfect 100 to 0 if Max Baucus of Montana, an ardent O'Connor supporter, had not had to return to his home state before the balloting. Even Jeremiah Denton, the only member of the Judiciary Committee who had refused to recommend O'Connor's confirmation, voted "yea" this time. He confessed that colleagues warned him they would "laugh me out of the Senate if I voted no."

Immediately she was surrounded by well-wishers. Barry Goldwater gave her a big hug. She was escorted outside to have her picture taken on the Capitol steps. She gazed at the imposing marble facade of the Supreme Court across the way and said, "My hope is that ten years from now, after I've been across the street and worked for a while, they'll feel glad that they gave me this wonderful vote."

Her friends were already giving her a vote of confidence. Judge Patricia Lamson of Phoenix says, "As a matter of fact, I know she can 'run rings' around the other justices. . . She has been an absolute inspiration to me. . . She is a most gracious lady with a delightful sense of humor, and her sharp legal mind and judicial temperament will make her an outstanding justice."

Carolyn Warner, Arizona State Superintendent of Public Instruction, explains her own feelings. "She had many opportunities to run for United States senator, representative, or governor. Because of her life's balance, she was reluctant to go to Washington. Her family spent a lot of time together when her sons were young and it would have been inconvenient to her husband and children to pull up their roots. But those were offices you seek. The Supreme Court is an office that seeks you. I think she sees it as a calling."

President Ronald Reagan and Chief Justice Warren Burger join Justice Sandra Day O'Connor immediately after the swearing-in ceremony.

—Wide World Photos

Her calling came at a perfect time. Sandra is most willing to admit she was in the right place at the right time. The President was looking for a qualified woman, a moderate conservative, and a Westerner if possible. Her own life had to have come full circle to fit into such a tremendous job.

Carolyn Warner commented, "She is a real person with an excellent mind. Her life is well structured and well organized, but she's not a caricature. She deals with her home, family and work demands in the same way without allowing one segment of her life to become overblown."

It was now time to let her career take first place in her life and in the life of her family. Now there was only the formal investiture and the "settling in" to be done.

This settling in meant pulling up stakes for the whole family. Although John O'Connor has been called a very supportive husband, there must have been difficult moments of decision. True, he is a very fine lawyer, senior partner in a large Phoenix law firm, but in no way could his career compare to the prestige of a judge, and surely not to the post of Supreme Court justice.

His wife's name was frequently in the press. She was continually called for interviews. Would he try to commute to Washington to be with his wife, or find a new position for himself? Without hesitation he gave up his Phoenix law practice. It takes a very secure, self-assured man to make such a major change.

Although he did not know it at the time he made the decision, a fine offer for a Washington, D.C., position came within the week. He is now affiliated with a prestigious firm specializing in tax law. He still cannot avoid the tag of being called the very first husband of a Supreme Court justice.

Their sons were launched on their own lives. In 1981, when their mother became a justice, Jay, age nineteen, was a freshman at Stanford, Brian was a junior at Colorado State, and Scott, the oldest at twenty-three, was in business in Phoenix with a real estate development company.

Sandra and John are true Westerners. Would a condominium on Embassy Row be able to substitute for

Sandra Day O'Connor and Chief Justice Warren Burger share a relaxed moment prior to the swearing-in ceremony.
—Wide World Photos

a spacious adobe home with memories? Those memories included friends and relatives they might not see for long periods of time. Adventures with Flournoy Davis Manzo and Betsy Taylor, who had known them when the children were growing up, would have to be shared in Washington now. And the miles to the Lazy B were more than a car could make for a spur-of-the-moment weekend.

Already her busy schedule had cut into the days they could enjoy at the ranch. She had told Ronald Reagan, "As far as I'm concerned, the best place to be is on a good cutting horse working cattle."

After her investiture, phone calls and congratulatory wires came in by the hundreds. There were parties and celebrations. At an elegant luncheon Nancy Thurmond, wife of the chairman of the Judiciary Committee, offered a toast to the new justice. "She's the best thing to come down the pike since Girl Scout cookies."

A few days later she attended a ceremony in the Rose Garden of the White House honoring federal, district, and appellate court judges, and Supreme Court justices. Looking intently at O'Connor, the President spoke these solemn words, "The nation demands of judges a wisdom that knows no time, has no prejudice, and wants no other reward."

11

The partying had come to an end. The work was to begin. The Court convened October 5, 1981. But before that Sandra O'Connor had to appoint a staff, move her office and her home, and start studying the list of cases to be considered in the upcoming session. Frequently it meant putting in a twelve-hour day.

She feels that she must prove herself absolutely without fault in dedication to her profession. She wants to change the opinions of some persons that she received her appointment only as a token to please leaders of the women's movement.

The nine justices work independently. Each year a justice may choose four clerks from the best of the nation's law school graduates to help prepare background research and statistics for the cases in question. Secretaries help sort and answer the mail under the justices' directions, and a messenger is assigned to each justice, but no amount of help can lessen O'Connor's responsibilities in her job.

Always a conscientious judge in studying the facts of cases before consideration, today she is driving herself almost beyond reason. Yet she seems to be thriving on this heavy schedule.

She has found that often she is up at four in the morning to tackle legal briefs before heading to her court office. On her desk there is a two-tiered in-basket for papers in need of her attention that is kept filled throughout the day. Her desk top is so big she keeps two pens in penholders at a far corner so she can jot a note without having to get back to her chair.

In spite of such a heavy schedule, she has organized an exercise class and has invited fifteen Supreme Court clerks and staffers to join her. She knows that health is important to her job.

What matters most in the long run about Sandra O'Connor is that she is the youngest justice in the Court. Five of her fellow justices are over seventy.

"Sandra is driven and can outwork them all," said a lawyer friend. "That gives her a tremendous advantage."

The Court's remaining liberals, William Brennan, Jr. and Thurgood Marshall, have been in poor health in the past, but neither will voluntarily resign. They hope to stay on until a more liberal President is elected, who in turn will choose more liberal replacements.

Justice Marshall has stated frequently with only the thinnest veneer of politeness that the majority of the Court are a bunch of rich, old white men incapable of understanding what life is like for those who are black and/or poor and/or female. Many people feel that the Court should mirror the society more closely in its membership. And certainly Justice O'Connor's appointment represents a step toward the broadening of the Court.

What is hard about interpreting the fundamental law of this country is that there are no formulas for making decisions. Such grand phrases as "equal protection" are not clearly defined. Much of the Constitution consists of concepts—"due process," "unreasonable searches"—that can only be given meaning in concrete cases. Judges try to stick only to the law, but the Supreme Court, more than any other court in the land, puts meaning into these grand words. Judges do make policy whether they want to or not.

The Supreme Court also influences laws by deciding which cases it will hear. In O'Connor's first session, over 1000 cases had piled up for consideration by the Court. Obviously not all of them could be heard. One of her first jobs was to participate in a week of closed-door discussions in which the justices decided what cases they would consider.

As in recent years, the justices were faced with difficult questions of bias in employment, education, and housing.

In several cases the Court had to decide which kinds

of job-seniority plans were immune from challenge as discriminatory—how to be fair to both the older employees not wanting to retire and to younger workers being kept from advancement because of no room "up the ladder."

Fair-housing advocates asked the Court's permission to sue landlords in antidiscriminatory suits using evidence gathered by "testers" who posed as potential buyers.

Other cases posed the issue of whether the federal government may deny aid to schools and colleges that practice employment bias—institutions that might exclusively hire members of a certain church group, for instance, or refuse to hire women or minorities in any but menial jobs.

Sandra O'Connor's first majority opinion for the Court concerned: *"Watt, Secretary of the Interior,* et al. v. *Energy Action Educational Foundation* et al." The Court ruled unanimously that the government does not have to make it easier for small companies to compete for offshore oil leases.

The justices take turns recording these decisions. If there are dissenting opinions they are written too. Sandra's seventeen-page summary of the problem with documented reasons for the conclusions drawn, was professional and meticulous. She was proving herself well. However, she warned her family that once the decision was made known her popularity would surely disappear. She wrote, "The honeymoon isn't over yet, but it is fast disappearing. Once the decision appears, it will be gone."

But, as she has said, "To be liked for every deed and word is to fail."

Among other decisions handed down by the Supreme Court since Sandra Day O'Connor became a member is one involving the right of children of illegal aliens to a free public school education. The Court ruled 5 to 4 that a 1977 Texas statute barring these children from public schools unless they paid a $1000 tuition was unconstitutional. The Court said that keeping the children of illegal aliens out of school was punishing the children for the wrongdoing of the parents. Such an idea went against a fundamental concept of justice.

A unanimous decision ruled that mentally retarded patients who had been involuntarily committed to state institutions have a constitutional right to safety and freedom of movement. They also have a right to training to help them to enjoy these rights. However, the rights must be balanced against factors such as protection of other patients. This ruling directly affects the approximately 135,000 retarded persons in institutions, and indirectly lends support to 6,000,000 other retarded citizens.

A well-publicized case involved censorship and school libraries. The school board from the Island

Margaret Kuhn, founder of the Gray Panthers, and Justice O'Connor received bouquets at the 1982 Gimbel Awards luncheon in Philadelphia.

—Wide World Photos

Trees Union Free School District of Long Island had removed nine books from the school libraries, saying that they were objectionable in various ways. Five students filed suit to have the books put back. A Federal District Court dismissed the suit without a trial. However, in a 5 to 4 decision, the Supreme Court ruled that local school boards may not remove books from school library shelves "simply because they dislike the ideas" contained in them. This cleared the way for the students to sue and to challenge the banning of books. As a result, the controversial books were returned to the libraries before the case went to court.

What has Sandra Day O'Connor's influence been on the Court? Her presence probably will not alter its ideological balance for some time. She replaced a justice who tended to side with conservatives on important issues, but who was known as a "centrist and swing man" who voted his conscience.

"Justice O'Connor is also a middle-roader, not an extreme rightist or leftist," said Phoenix lawyer David C. Tierney. "She will make her own way and be her own person."

In Sandra Day O'Connor's first year on the Supreme Court she took part in 139 decisions. Although she sided most often with the conservative side of the Court, on occasion she voted with the senior liberal spokesman, Justice William J. Brennan, Jr. Justice O'Connor joined a 6 to 3 majority opinion by Justice Blackmun that a Federal law known as Title IX does prohibit employment discrimination in educational institutions that receive Federal funds.

Again voting with Justice Brennan in an important discrimination case, Justice O'Connor wrote a 5 to 4 majority opinion saying that a Mississippi state school of nursing for women could not constitutionally refuse to admit male students. In writing this opinion, she looked at discrimination from the point of view of the male applicant, and from the fact that the women nursing students were being stereotyped by the restricted admissions policy. She even devoted a footnote to Myra Bradwell, an Illinois woman who had been rejected by the Supreme Court in her plea to practice law some 110 years ago. Justice O'Connor quoted the Court's words of refusal at the time—about the "peculiar characteristics, destiny and mission of woman."

12

People are asking what effect Sandra Day O'Connor's appointment will have on the women's movement. Has she opened the door for more young women to enter the legal profession?

The answer here is a firm yes. As a modern woman, she is a flawless example, melding family, career, and civic responsibilities. She has not let prejudice stop her. She has proved herself to be a woman with an eye for traditional values, but with a determination to break tradition to carve out new opportunities in her profession.

She has the will and ability to communicate reform in a moderate way that is more easily accepted. She has quietly succeeded by speaking softly with intelligence and logic.

"We're hoping she won't be considered a token nomination to appease the rest of us," said Eleanor

Smeal, President of the National Organization for Women.

With the increase in numbers of women in law, pressure is bound to increase to prevent this from happening.

Although long since overdue, women have been making strides in the legal profession. Only about 3 percent of the lawyers in the 1950s and 1960s were women. In 1968 there were three women among the hundreds of partners in large Wall Street firms. These are the most powerful law firms in the country. Only 5 percent of judges in federal district courts and courts of appeals were women. Most women judges were to be found in municipal courts or held posts as justices of the peace. These figures are now changing.

In 1981 there were forty-one women partners in Wall Street firms, most having been promoted since 1975. In the fifty largest firms in the United States, in New York, Chicago, Houston, Cleveland, Omaha, and San Francisco, 21.5 percent of the lawyers were women. Lawsuits against the large firms also resulted in settlements that guaranteed qualified women jobs and promotions. The percentage of women law students rose from 4 percent in 1970 to 33 percent in the early 1980s.

When asked how she wanted to be remembered, Sandra O'Connor said she would be satisfied with a tombstone that read, "Here lies a good judge."

Because of her special status she will never be regarded as just another justice. She probably will be measured, at least initially, against the Court's other firsts: Roger Taney, the first Catholic, who wrote the Dred Scott decision that said slaves could be considered as property; Louis Brandeis, the first Jew and one of the extraordinary legal minds of the century; and Thurgood Marshall, the first black, whose votes on civil rights cases before the Court helped make major changes in our society.

Sandra O'Connor's very presence on the Court is a symbol of the change in women's status in the twentieth century. One hundred and eight years ago Justice Charles C. Nott ruled against another woman, Belva Ann Lockwood, who had petitioned for the right to hear cases before the Court as a lawyer.

The motion was simple. "A married woman, domiciled in the District of Columbia, and admitted to practice as an attorney in the highest court of the District, applies for admission to the bar of this court."

The opinion of the Court was equally simple. There was no statutory law and no precedent for the plea. A married woman attorney might conceivably misapply funds of a client, and under the common law her husband might be sued for the wrong which she had committed as an attorney. Justice Nott doubted the merits of permitting women "to enter the fierce battle of modern competition."

He delivered the following opinion of the court: "A woman is without legal capacity to take the office of attorney." It took an act of Congress to reverse this decision.

In a commencement address at Stanford University, Justice O'Connor spoke of individual responsibility and indicated that people need to work out their own problems without resorting to the overburdened courts. She cited an ancient saying: " 'In every age, there comes a time when leadership suddenly comes forth to meet the needs of the hour. And so there is no man who does not find his time, and there is no hour that does not have its leader.' "

Justice O'Connor continued: "Whether we will lead only a family, or a handful of friends, and where and how we will lead is up to us, our views and our talents... But the hour will come for each of us, and because of this, we surely must also know that the very nature of humanity and society, regardless of its size or complexity, will always turn on the act of the individual and, therefore, on the quality of that individual.

"My experience in the executive, legislative and judicial branches of government and my position on the Supreme Court all point to this conclusion: an informed, reasoned effort by one citizen can have dramatic impact on how someone, like a legislator, will vote and act."

She stated further, "One of the things each of you can do as individuals to improve our nation's court system is to help us resolve more of the disputes which arise in this country someplace other than in the courtroom."

Justice O'Connor firmly believes that the courts are carrying too large a burden and that we can't solve the problem by appointing more judges.

She suggests that "...as you negotiate disputes, you remember the golden rule: do unto others what you would have them do unto you. That might make you a little more generous, save you a lot of time and money and make my job a lot easier."

The U.S. Supreme Court, 1982.

INDEX